Animal  Adaptations

Symbiosis

JACK ZAYARNY

MEDIA ENHANCED BOOKS

AV²
BY WEIGL

ADDED VALUE · AUDIO VISUAL

www.av2books.com

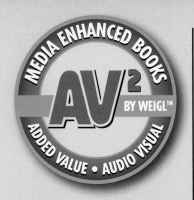

AV² provides enriched content that supplements and complements this book. Weigl's AV² books strive to create inspired learning and engage young minds in a total learning experience.

Your AV² Media Enhanced books come alive with...

Audio
Listen to sections of the book read aloud.

Key Words
Study vocabulary, and complete a matching word activity.

Video
Watch informative video clips.

Quizzes
Test your knowledge.

Embedded Weblinks
Gain additional information for research.

Slide Show
View images and captions, and prepare a presentation.

Try This!
Complete activities and hands-on experiments.

... and much, much more!

Go to **www.av2books.com**, and enter this book's unique code.

BOOK CODE

W 3 2 8 0 0

AV² by Weigl brings you media enhanced books that support active learning.

Published by AV² by Weigl
350 5th Avenue, 59th Floor
New York, NY 10118
Website: www.av2books.com   www.weigl.com

Library of Congress Cataloguing in Publication data available upon request.
Fax 1-866-449-3445 for the attention of the Publishing Records department.

ISBN 978-1-4896-1386-8 (hardcover)
ISBN 978-1-4896-1387-5 (softcover)
ISBN 978-1-4896-1388-2 (single-user eBook)
ISBN 978-1-4896-1389-9 (multi-user eBook)

Printed in the United States of America in North Mankato, Minnesota
1 2 3 4 5 6 7 8 9 18 17 16 15 14

062014
WEP050914

Project Coordinator Aaron Carr
Art Director Terry Paulhus

Every reasonable effort has been made to trace ownership and to obtain permission to reprint copyright material. The publishers would be pleased to have any errors or omissions brought to their attention so that they may be corrected in subsequent printings.

Photo Credits
Weigl acknowledges Getty Images as its primary photo supplier for this title.

Contents

What Is an Adaptation?

Many animals have **features** that allow them to survive better in their **habitat**. **Natural selection** is a process by which the features of these surviving animals are passed on to their offspring. These features are known as adaptations.

Adaptations develop over a long time, usually over thousands of years. Being able to survive in heat or cold, fast movement, and color are some examples of adaptations that help animals survive changing conditions.

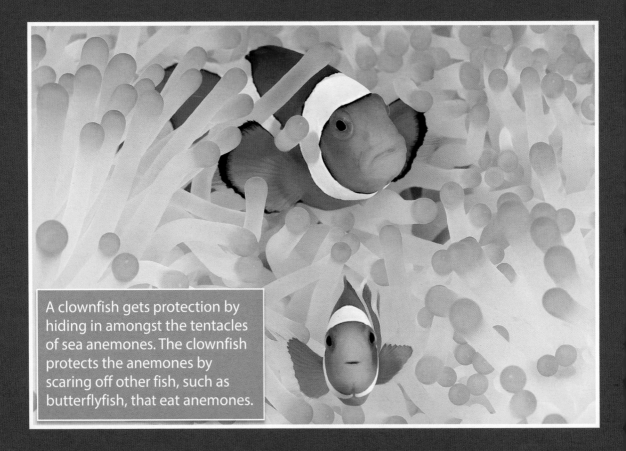

A clownfish gets protection by hiding in amongst the tentacles of sea anemones. The clownfish protects the anemones by scaring off other fish, such as butterflyfish, that eat anemones.

Changes in the food sources of ants over 50 million years ago caused them to begin "farming" small insects called aphids. Aphids feed on plant sap and produce a highly nutritious **nectar** known as "honeydew." Ants gather and feed on this nectar, keeping aphids close to their nests. In return, the aphids are protected from **predators** by the ant colony. This is known as a symbiotic relationship. This relationship is passed down to the offspring of ants and aphids. It helps them both survive.

Ants protect aphids from predators. In return, aphids produce honeydew, which ants eat.

What Is Symbiosis?

Symbiosis is a relationship between two different **species** where at least one species benefits. Sometimes both species benefit greatly and other times one species may benefit but the other species could be harmed. There are two main types of symbiosis. *Ectosymbiosis* is when a species interacts with the outside body of another species. *Endosymbiosis* happens when one species lives within the body of another species, such as in the bloodstream.

ECTOSYMBIOSIS

A bee gets nectar from flowers which can later be turned into honey. Pollen from the flowers sticks to the hairs on the bee's body. When the bee flies to the next flower, pollen from the first flower is able to **fertilize** the second flower. This relationship provides a food source for the bee and helps the flowers **reproduce**.

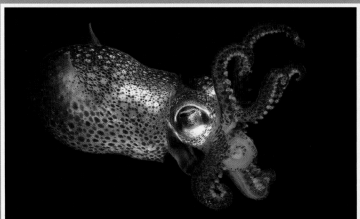

ENDOSYMBIOSIS

The bobtail squid has **bacteria** living in its body that glows. This light allows the squid to hunt in the dark. The bacteria gets its food from the squid's most recent catch.

Symbiotic Adaptations in Animals

One of the most important symbiotic relationships in all of nature is within human and animal bodies. *Mitochondria* are cells which produce energy within a body. However, they did not begin as a single unit. More than a billion years ago, a bacteria tried to consume another, smaller variation of a microorganism. However, the prey bacteria survived within the body of its predator. Over millions of years, this "guest" bacteria began to live within the protected and nutrient-rich environment of its host.

Throughout this time, the smaller bacteria adapted and learned to change nutrients and oxygen into chemical energy for both itself and its host. Then, both species survived. It is thought that, in time, this symbiotic relationship became the base for all cell life in human and animal bodies.

Mitochondria are the cell's power producers. They convert energy into forms that are usable by the cell.

What Does It Do?

Symbiosis creates relationships that exist outside of a standard **food web**. These relationships allow the species to gain food, shelter, or protection from disease or pests.

Sometimes this relationship is key to the survival of one or both species. In other cases, the benefit might be small or not necessary for the species to survive. The relationship depends on the species involved, their environment, and the length of time over which the symbiotic relationship has been developed.

Groupers feed on pygmy sweepers, but only sometimes. They also protect pygmy fish from other predators, in effect "farming" their own food.

The Ocean Floor Food Web

A series of food chains develops on the ocean floor. These involve symbiotic relationships. Algae work together with **coral** to make energy for both species. The coral makes carbon dioxide that the algae can use. Cleaner fish eat algae, but hide in the coral reefs to escape their predators. Large fish that usually feed on smaller fish use these areas to rid themselves of **parasites**. When all these creatures die, the energy from their remains is used by the algae. This restarts the process.

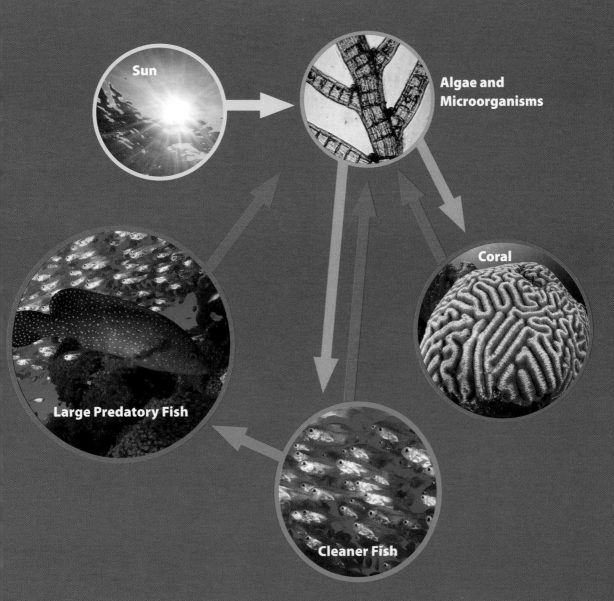

Sun

Algae and Microorganisms

Coral

Large Predatory Fish

Cleaner Fish

Types of Symbiosis

The three main types of symbiotic relationships are called *mutualism, commensalism,* and *parasitism.*

In mutualism, both species benefit from the relationship. The relationship between clownfish and anemones is an example of mutualism. In commensalism, the relationship has no impact on one species but benefits the other. For example, a bird living on a tree has little or no impact on the health of the tree, but the bird gains shelter and protection. Parasitism is when one species benefits from the relationship and the other species is harmed by it. The harming organism is known as a parasite. The parasite may spread disease to the host animal in exchange for food or shelter.

A flea is a parasite that uses an animal's blood for its food. It can pass diseases from one animal to another.

Mutualism

Ostriches and zebras often herd together. Zebras have poor eyesight, while ostriches have poor smell and hearing. By staying together, each species can alert the other of approaching predators.

Commensalism

A cattle egret is a kind of bird that follows herds of mammals, such as cows. The cow's hooves dig up worms and insects as it walks. The egret can eat these. Cows are unaffected by this relationship, while the egret benefits.

Parasitism

A tapeworm gets food and shelter from an animal. The animal experiences harm because tapeworms live within its body and take nutrients away from it.

How Does It Work?

Symbiotic relationships appear to be "perfect", but they are actually adaptations that have developed over millions of years. Though one or both species may benefit from the relationship, the plant, animal, or fungus does not, in most cases, choose to help the other species. Rather, the interaction between the two is driven by **instinct**. Instinct is a behavior that an organism naturally displays. For example, birds have the instinct to build nests. In symbiosis, the species benefiting from the relationship is more likely to be healthy. A healthy animal is more likely to have healthy offspring, passing on genes that give them similar instincts.

Building a nest is an instinct that bird species pass from one generation to the next.

4 EXAMPLES OF SYMBIOSIS

Domestic Animals

Modern dogs developed from wolves that had behaviors that could be trained by humans. These included herding, the ability to follow commands, and loyalty. Humans gained protection from these early dogs and the dogs gained food and shelter.

Trees

For thousands of years, trees have used a kind of fungi to get vitamins and minerals needed for **photosynthesis**. The fungi, in exchange, received food in the form of sugar from the tree after photosynthesis.

Human Body

The human digestive system contains several hundred different kinds of bacteria. This bacteria allows the body to break food down into smaller pieces. This process results in the production of vitamins and minerals which the human body uses. The bacteria receives a direct food source.

Flowers

Many flowers have become brighter in color over time and have begun to produce a sweet nectar that attracts hummingbirds. In turn, hummingbirds receive a high-energy food source, while also delivering pollen to other flowers and assisting them in reproduction.

Timeline

In the animal kingdom, the process of natural selection is necessary to ensure the survival of a species. **Traits** such as symbiosis help certain members of the species adapt better to a changing environment. These members survive longer and pass on their adaptive traits to their offspring. A trait-like symbiosis can be gradually developed and passed on among the species for millions of years. It allows animals that have it to reproduce more successfully.

Orange rat snake

Yellow rat snake

Green rat snake

Rat snakes are found in many different colors. This is because they have adapted to their local environments and can camouflage themselves for both hunting and for protection.

Canine-Human Symbiosis Timeline

20,000 Years Ago

Humans and wolves both hunted large animals. The two species shared their prey and learned to work together.

12,000 Years Ago

Wolf pups adopted by humans began to live in human settlements. These first dogs were bred for certain qualities such as loyalty and obedience.

Today

There are about 493 different breeds of dog in the world. They have become great human companions. This is an example of mutualism, a symbiotic relationship that benefits both.

Copying Symbiosis

Human relationships are full of symbiosis. People frequently rely on each other to fulfill a need or perform a task. A farmer selling to a customer is an example of a mutually beneficial symbiotic relationship. The farmer receives money and the customer receives food. On a larger scale, symbiosis also happens between organizations, companies, and even governments and nations. For example, a transport company relies on its suppliers to stay in business, and its suppliers rely on the transport company to deliver goods to its customers.

Human symbiotic relationships can have many different stages. Vegetables and fruit are delivered to a stall-holder. The stall-holder then juices the product, packages it, and sells it to a customer.

Bees are given shelter, protection, and care. Beekeepers are rewarded with a high-quality product at no harm to the bees.

Symbiotic relationships between humans and the natural world have always been important to people such as **environmentalists** and **conservationists**. **Sustainable** agriculture, nature parks, and wildlife areas are all important to establishing mutually beneficial relationships. Industries such as beekeeping are an example of a successful symbiotic relationship between humans and animals.

Symbiosis and Biodiversity

Biodiversity is the word used to describe the variety of animals, plants, and other natural elements in a habitat. A large variety of different animals and plants allows an environment to work properly. Every organism has a role to play in the food web. They all depend on each other for nutrition, shelter, oxygen, and reproduction.

Symbiosis is an important part of biodiversity. It is a common adaptation in plants, animals, and other small organisms. It can be said to be one of the building blocks of life. Symbiotic relationships contribute to biodiversity by changing the development of species and creating variety.

Sea anemones "ride" with hermit crabs to areas where there is more food.

Large fish are "cleaned" by smaller fish. This symbiotic relationship has developed so that the larger fish is able to give off signals promising not to eat its "cleaners."

The red-billed oxpecker feeds on the back of large animals. It cleans the animal of ticks and parasites, but it also feeds on its blood.

Conservation

Natural environments are finely balanced systems. Upsetting this balance will often lead to harm for one or more species in the environment. Destruction of trees, land, and natural cover upsets symbiotic relationships. Damaging or changing the environment can cause one half of a symbiotic relationship to suffer. This could damage the survival of both species. The lack of balance harms biodiversity and puts the survival of many species in danger. To avoid this, many organizations work to protect wildlife environments. Conservation groups such as the **International Union for Conservation of Nature (IUCN)** and ranger services for national parks play a central role in the preservation of our natural environment.

Cutting down trees can cause problems to the systems within an environment.

Activity

Using this book and other sources, describe in your own words how symbiosis works.

Then, match each animal with its partner in a symbiotic relationship.

1 Impala

2 Sea Anemone

3 Flowering Plants

Great White Shark 4

Algae 5

6 Aphids

Remora Fish

A

B

African Oxpecker

C Clownfish

Coral

D

Ant

E

F

Bee

Answers: 1.B 2.C 3.F 4.A 5.D 6.E

Quiz

Complete this quiz to test your knowledge of symbiosis.

1 What is the role of adaptations?

A. They give an animal the ability to be better in a certain function.

2 What animal produces a nectar called "honeydew" that is consumed by ants?

A. An aphid.

3 What are the two types of symbiosis?

A. Ectosymbiosis and endosymbiosis.

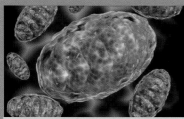

4 What is the name of the cell that formed as a result of a symbiotic relationship?

A. Mitochondria.

5 How does a grouper fish "farm" its own food?

A. It protects pygmy fish from other predators.

6 What are the three main types of symbiotic relationships?

A. Mutualism, commensalism, parasitism.

7 What is instinct?

A. A behavior developed from the natural biological drive of the species.

8 How many different types of bacteria does the human body contain?

A. Several hundred

9 How many years ago did the first domesticated dogs appear?

A. 12,000 years

10 Why is the small fish not eaten by the larger fish while it is "cleaning"?

A. The large fish gives off "protection" signals.

Key Words

bacteria: very small organisms unable to be seen by the human eye. Some bacteria are beneficial, some are not.

conservationists: individuals or organizations with the goal of protecting the natural environment

coral: a rock-like substance made from the bodies of marine plants

environmentalists: individuals who care about looking after the environment

features: characteristics of an object or living creature

fertilize: provide nutrients to allow something to grow

food web: a system of interactions between living things

habitat: the natural environment of a living thing

instinct: a fixed pattern of behaviour that happens naturally

International Union for Conservation of Nature (IUCN): an organization that works to solve a number of environmental issues worldwide

natural selection: a natural process where animals that have better adapted to their environment survive and pass on those adaptations to their young

nectar: nutritious liquid composed mainly of sugar

parasites: organisms that live on and gets nutrients from the body of another, unwilling organism

photosynthesis: the process used by plants to convert light into chemical energy

predators: animals that hunt and eat other animals

reproduce: to make another one of the same kind

species: a group of plants or animals that are alike in many ways

sustainable: able to be kept at a certain level

traits: special characteristics

Index

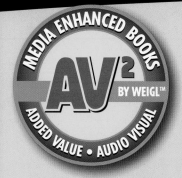

Log on to www.av2books.com

AV² by Weigl brings you media enhanced books that support active learning. Go to www.av2books.com, and enter the special code found on page 2 of this book. You will gain access to enriched and enhanced content that supplements and complements this book. Content includes video, audio, weblinks, quizzes, a slide show, and activities.

AV² Online Navigation

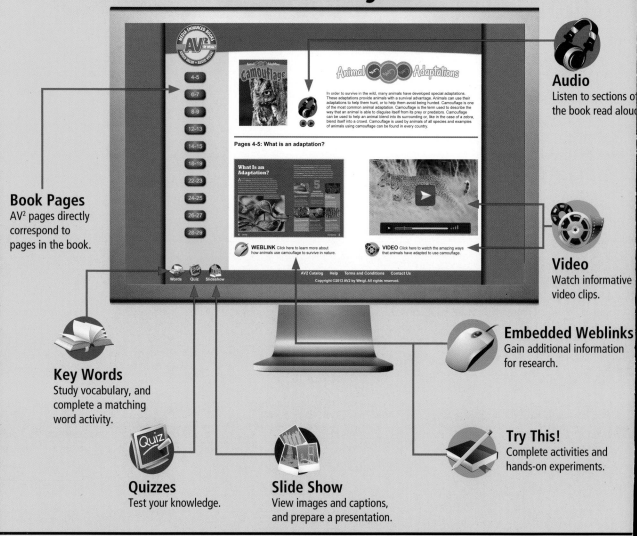

Audio
Listen to sections of the book read aloud

Book Pages
AV² pages directly correspond to pages in the book.

Video
Watch informative video clips.

Key Words
Study vocabulary, and complete a matching word activity.

Embedded Weblinks
Gain additional information for research.

Try This!
Complete activities and hands-on experiments.

Quizzes
Test your knowledge.

Slide Show
View images and captions, and prepare a presentation.

AV² was built to bridge the gap between print and digital. We encourage you to tell us what you like and what you want to see in the future.

Sign up to be an AV² Ambassador at www.av2books.com/ambassador.

Due to the dynamic nature of the internet, some of the URLs and activities provided as part of AV² by Weigl may have changed or ceased to exist. AV² by Weigl accepts no responsibility for any such changes. All media enhanced books are regularly monitored to update addresses and sites in a timely manner. Contact AV² by Weigl at 1-866-649-3445 or av2books@weigl.com with any questions, comments, or feedback.